SPECTRUM®
EARLY YEARS

Basic Beginnings
EARLY WRITING
PRACTICE

Published by Spectrum®
an imprint of Carson-Dellosa Publishing LLC
Greensboro, NC

Spectrum
An imprint of Carson-Dellosa Publishing, LLC
P.O. Box 35665
Greensboro, NC 27425-5665

carsondellosa.com

ISBN 978-1-60996-886-1   01-044127784

Table of Contents

Welcome to *Basic Beginnings*

Basic Beginnings is a creative and developmentally appropriate series designed to fuel your child's learning potential. The early years of your child's life are bursting with cognitive and physical development. Therefore, it is essential to prepare your child for the basic skills and fine motor skills that are emphasized in the 21st century classroom. Basic skills include concepts such as recognizing letters, numbers, colors, shapes, and identifying same, different, and sequences of events. Fine motor skills are movements produced by small muscles or muscle groups, such as the precise hand movements required to write, cut, glue, and color. A child in preschool spends a lot of his or her day developing these muscles.

Basic Beginnings approaches learning through a developmentally appropriate process—ensuring your child is building the best foundation possible for preschool. Each activity is unique and fun, and stimulates your child's fine motor skills, hand-eye coordination, and ability to follow directions. Help your child complete the activities in this book. Each activity includes simple, step-by-step instructions. Provide your child with pencils, crayons, scissors, and glue for the various and creative activities he or she is about to discover.

Each book also includes three cutout mini books that reinforce the concepts your child is learning. You and your child will enjoy reading these simple stories together. Your child can make each story his or her own by coloring it, cutting it out, and, with your help, stapling the story together. Allow him or her to share the stories with you and others. Your child will begin to recognize sight words, hear vowel sounds, and understand sequences of events as he or she shares these delightful stories. With *Basic Beginnings*, the learning is never confined to the pages!

Early Writing Practice

Introduction to *Early Writing Practice*

Learning how to print can either be a frustrating and challenging experience for a young child, or it can be a fun and successful experience. All the activities in *Early Writing Practice* are designed to make learning how to print a fun and successful experience.

So, what makes the difference? Often, teachers and parents present learning how to print letters in alphabetical sequence. Developmentally, this is not ideal. A child needs to learn how to control a pencil and how to make various handwriting strokes before he or she is able to print letters. *Early Writing Practice* provides your child with the opportunity to learn how to control a pencil and then learn specific handwriting strokes, which then enables him or her to print a variety of alphabet letters. For example, in *Early Writing Practice*, your child first learns how to make tall straight lines and then long straight lines. When a child is able to complete these lines he or she is able to print the letters: **l, i, L, t, T, F, E, H,** and **I**. Your child is learning correct handwriting skills and will immediately feel successful.

The strokes taught in *Early Writing Practice* are as follows:

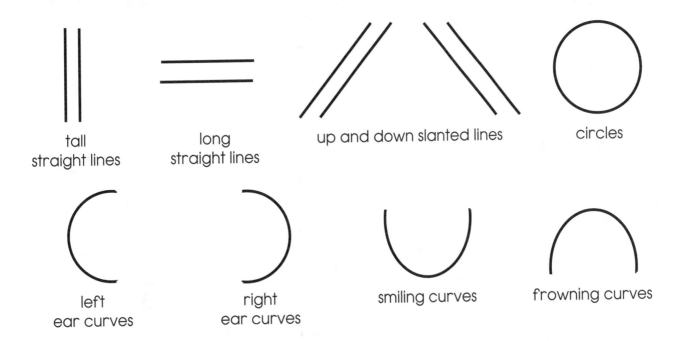

| tall straight lines | long straight lines | up and down slanted lines | circles |
| left ear curves | right ear curves | smiling curves | frowning curves |

Extra Ideas to Strengthen Fine Motor Skills

A young child needs a large variety of experiences to strengthen fine motors skills and to learn how to print. Finger painting, modeling with play dough, opening and closing clothespins, using scissors and snipping the edges of paper, pegboards, and beading are all wonderful activities that build small muscle strength and coordination.

Writing Checklist

Your child has mastered the following nine strokes necessary for learning how to print:

- ❏ tall straight lines
- ❏ long straight lines
- ❏ slanted up lines
- ❏ slanted down lines
- ❏ circles
- ❏ left ear strokes
- ❏ right ear strokes
- ❏ smiling strokes
- ❏ frowning strokes

Your child is able to print the following letters:

tall and long straight lines
- ❏ l
- ❏ i
- ❏ L
- ❏ T
- ❏ t
- ❏ F
- ❏ E
- ❏ H
- ❏ I

slanted lines
- ❏ V
- ❏ v
- ❏ W
- ❏ w
- ❏ N
- ❏ M
- ❏ Z
- ❏ z
- ❏ X
- ❏ x
- ❏ A
- ❏ Y
- ❏ y
- ❏ K
- ❏ k

circles
- ❏ O
- ❏ o
- ❏ Q

left ear curves
- ❏ C
- ❏ c
- ❏ G
- ❏ e
- ❏ a
- ❏ d
- ❏ g
- ❏ q

right ear curves
- ❏ D
- ❏ P
- ❏ R
- ❏ B
- ❏ p
- ❏ b

left and right ear curves
- ❏ S
- ❏ s

smiling curves
- ❏ U
- ❏ u
- ❏ J
- ❏ j

frowning curves
- ❏ n
- ❏ m
- ❏ r
- ❏ h
- ❏ f

Draw Tall Straight Lines

Directions: Start at each • and draw tall straight lines. Color the pencils.

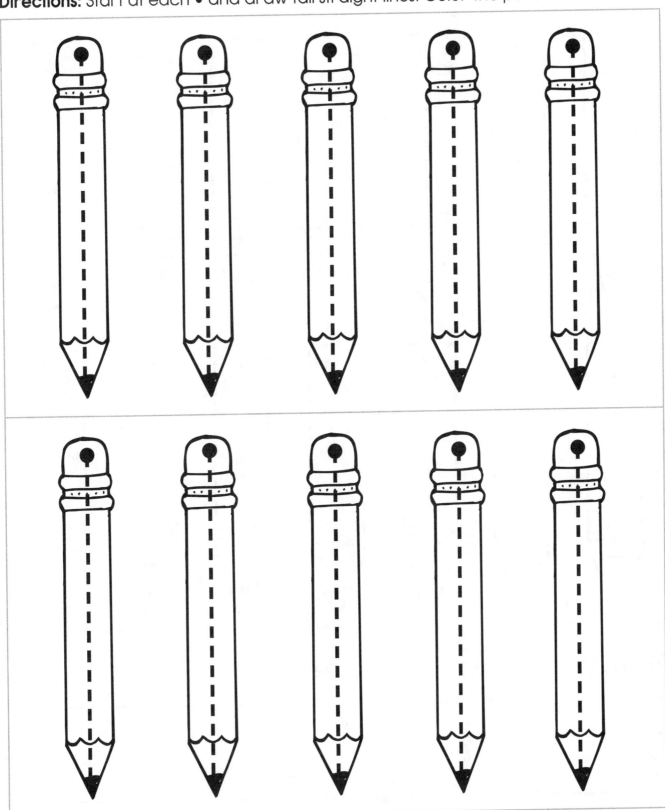

Early Writing Practice

Color Crayons

Directions: Start at each • and draw tall straight lines. Color the crayons.

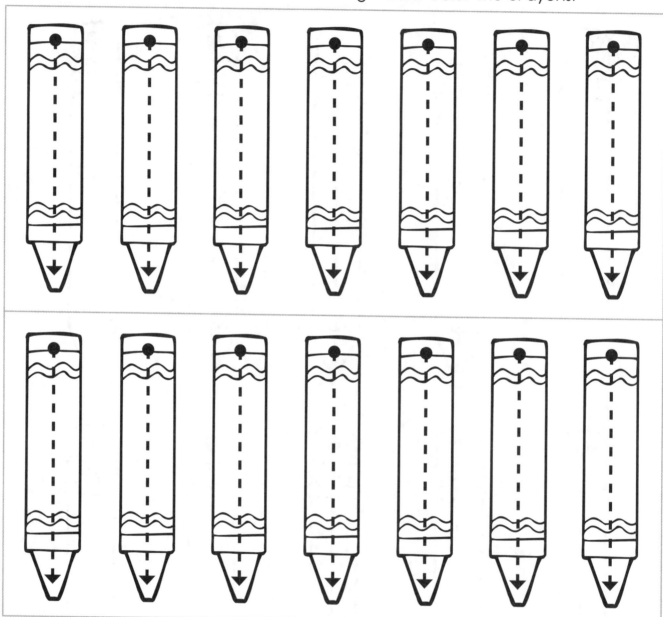

Now, you can write the letter l.

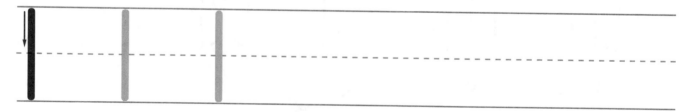

Early Writing Practice

Match the Same Pictures

Directions: Start at each • and draw tall straight lines.

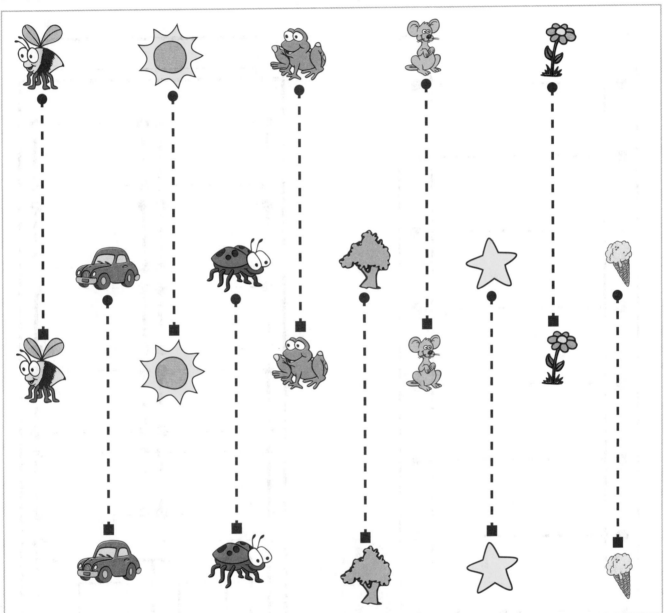

Now, you can write the letter i.

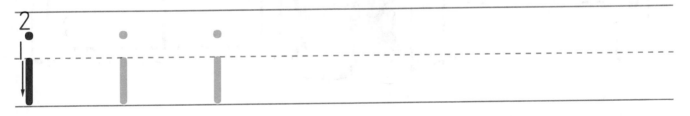

9

Draw Long Straight Lines

Directions: Trace the dotted lines to draw long straight lines. Color the picture.

Early Writing Practice

Help the Cat Get Back Home!

Directions: Start at the • and draw tall and long straight lines. Then, color the picture.

Now, you can write the letters L and T.

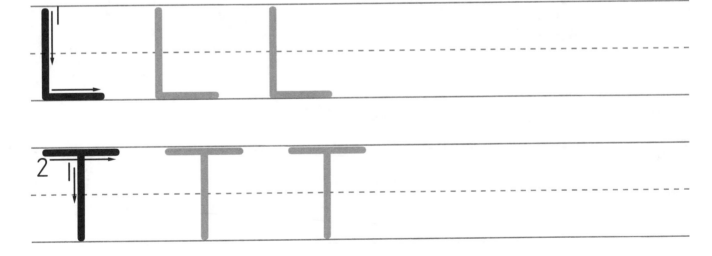

Early Writing Practice

Kites in the Sky

Directions: Draw lines to finish the kites. Then, color the kites.

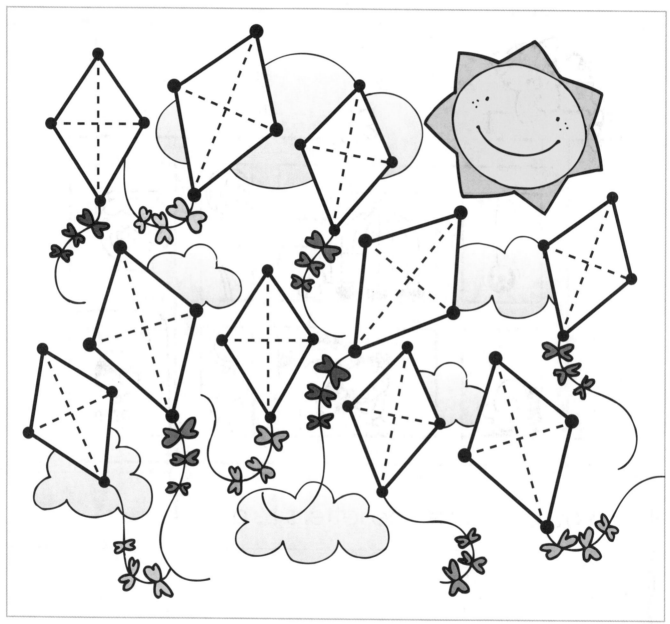

Now, you can write the letter **t**.

Dot-to-Dot City

Directions: Start at number 1 and draw tall and long straight lines. Color the picture.

Now, you can write the letters F and E.

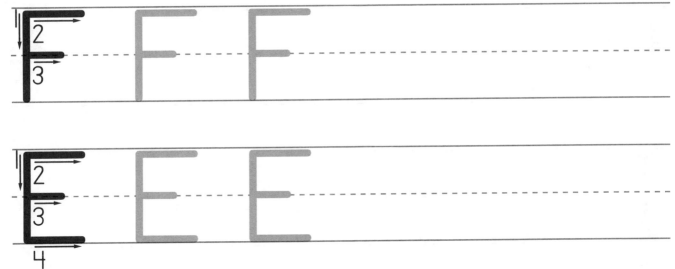

Copy Cat Letters

Directions: Be a copy cat. Trace and write the letters.

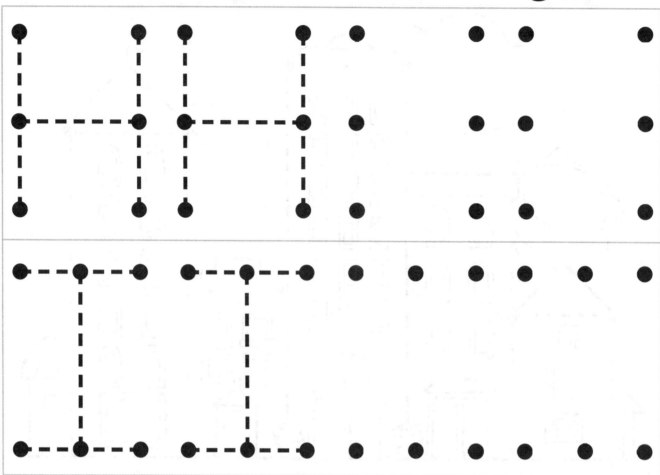

Now, you can write the letters H and I.

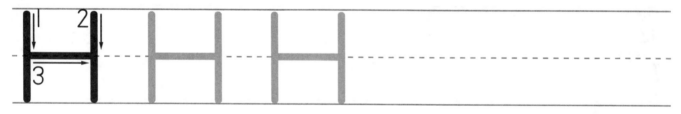

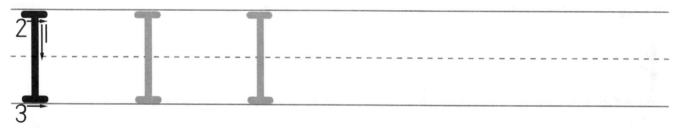

Early Writing Practice

Draw Up Slanted Lines

Directions: Start at each • and draw up slanted lines. Then, color the picture.

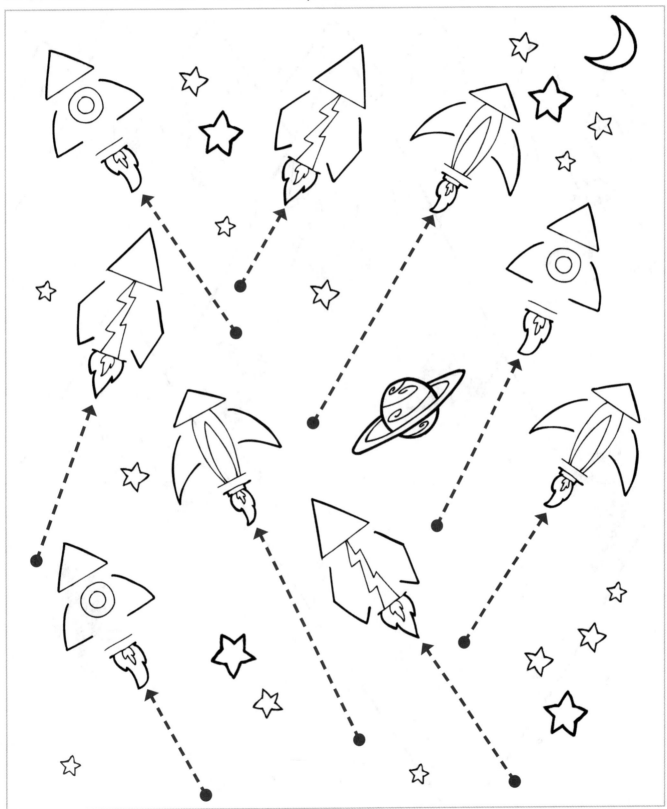

15

Draw Down Slanted Lines

Directions: Start at each • and draw down slanted lines.

Early Writing Practice

Finish the Leaves

Directions: Start at each • and trace the slanted lines. Then, color the picture.

Now, you can write the letters V and v.

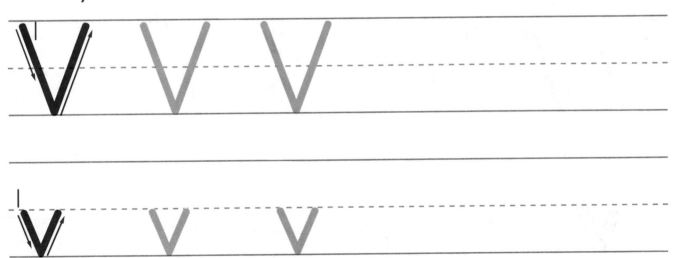

Early Writing Practice

Finish the Picture

Directions: Look at the example. Draw lines to make your hot air balloon look the same. Then, color both balloons.

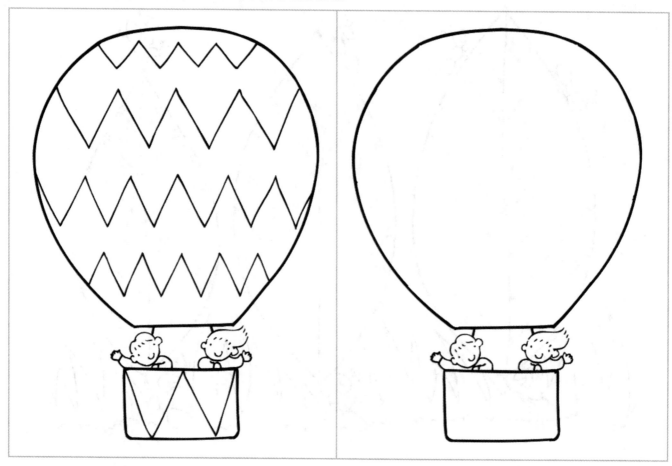

Now, you can write the letters **W** and **w**.

Early Writing Practice

Help the Bird Get to Her Nest

Directions: Draw down and up slanted lines.

Now, you can write the letter N.

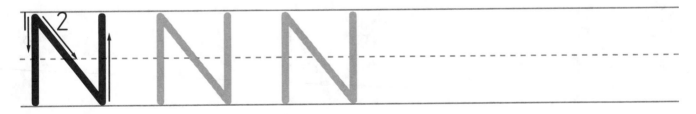

Early Writing Practice

The Mountain Man

Directions: Connect the •s to get the man over the mountains and color.

Now, you can write the letter M.

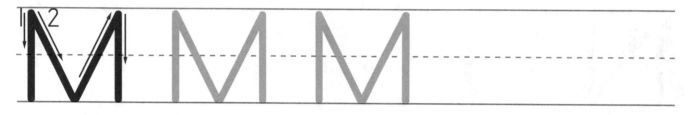

Early Writing Practice

Zig-Zag Goals!

Directions: Trace the lines to get the soccer players to the correct goals.

Now, you can write the letters Z and z.

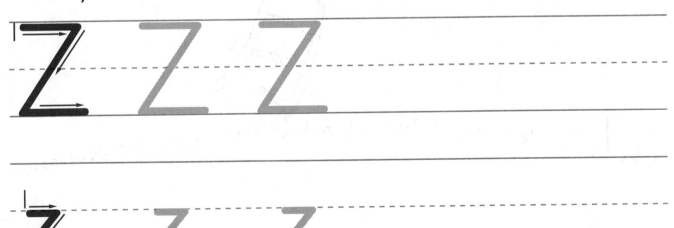

My Own Tree House

Directions: Draw a tree house using tall, long, and slanted lines. Color the picture.

22

2

Zip, zap, zig, zag, zoom!

4

Again,
zip, zap, zig, zag, zoom!

1

Zoie's Zippy Toy

3

Zoie, what is that
noise in your room?

23

6

Again,
zip, zap, zig, zag, zoom!

8

Notes to Parents

Directions: First, ask your child to color the mini book. Then, help him or her cut along the dotted lines. Next, have your child arrange the pages in the correct order. Staple the pages together. Read the story out loud to your child.

Extension ideas:
1. Have your child look at the text and circle each uppercase **Z** and lowercase **z**.
2. Read each **Zz** word with your child: **zip**, **zippy**, **zap**, **zag**, **zig**, **zoom**, **Zoie**, **Zoie-bot**.
3. Sing *Zip-a-dee Doo-dah*, and *We're Going to the Zoo.*
4. Make a zigzag hopscotch.
5. Ask your child to tell a story about his or her favorite toy.

5

Zoie, what is that
noise in your room?

7

I built a Zoie-bot
to clean my room.

25

Snowflakes

Directions: Connect the •s to make snowflakes.

Now, you can write the letters **X** and **x** .

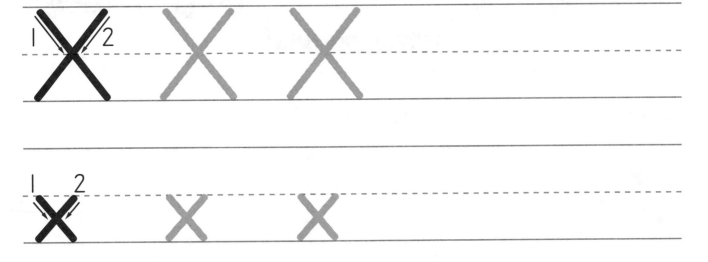

Early Writing Practice

Party Hats

Directions: Connect the •s to make party hats. Color the hats.

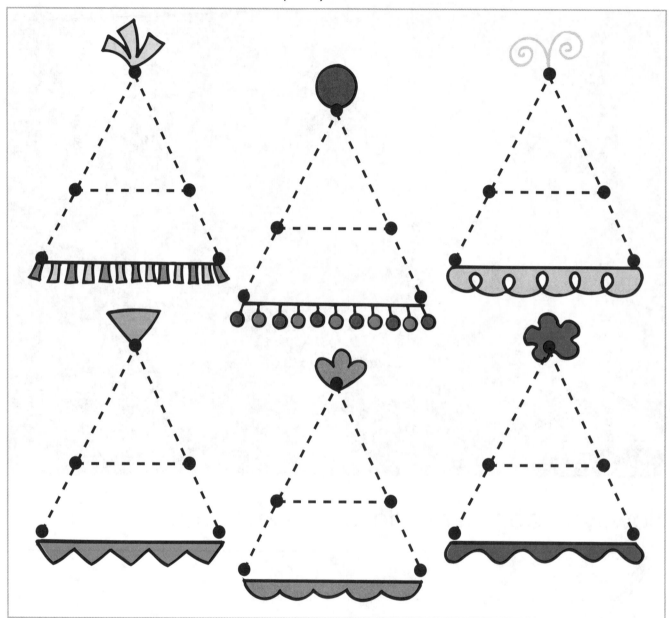

Now, you can write the letter A.

Early Writing Practice

"Y" Guys

Directions: Connect the •s to make the **Y** Guys.

Now, you can write the letters Y and y.

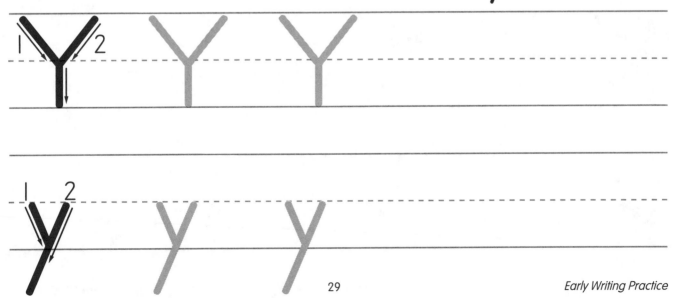

29

Singing Chicks

Directions: Connect the •s to make the chicks. Color the chicks.

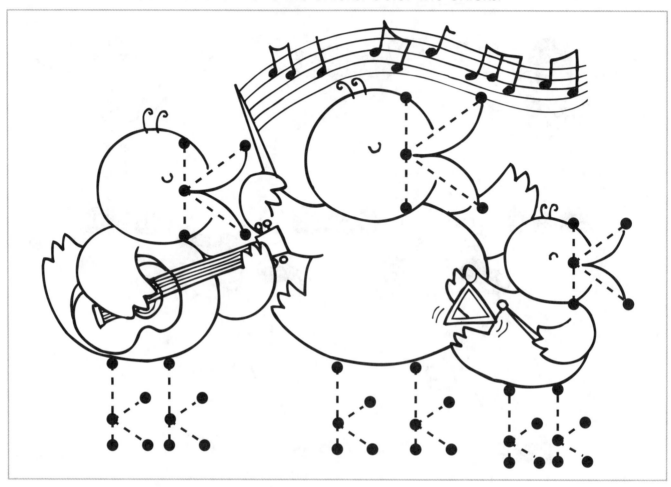

Now, you can write the letters K and k.

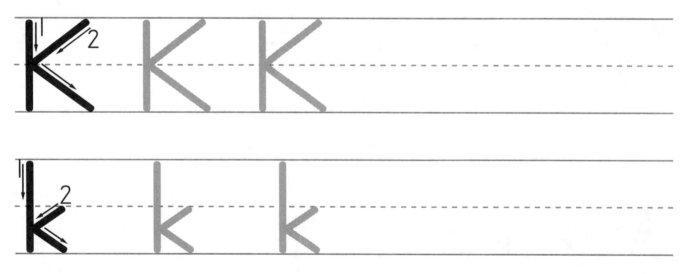

Draw Circles

Directions: Trace the circles on the pizza. Color the pizza.

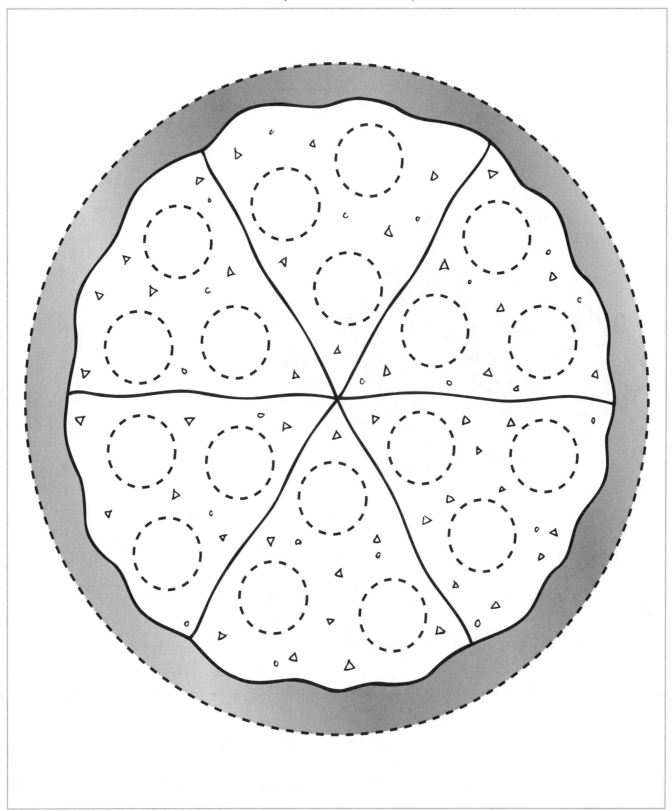

31

Blowing Bubbles

Directions: Draw your own bubbles.

Now, you can write the letters O and o.

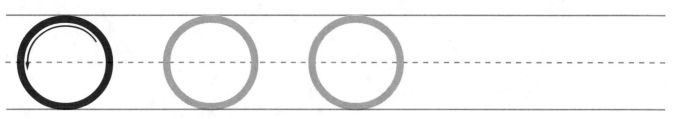

Early Writing Practice

Barnyard Chicks

Directions: Trace and color the chicks.

Now, you can write the letter Q.

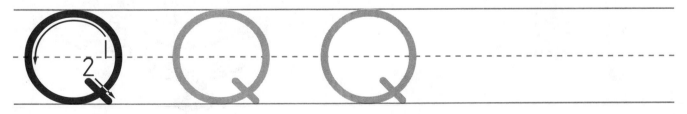

Draw Left Ear Strokes

Directions: Start at the • and trace the left ear strokes.

Early Writing Practice

Finish the Animals

Directions: Trace the left ear curves to finish the animals. Then, color the animals.

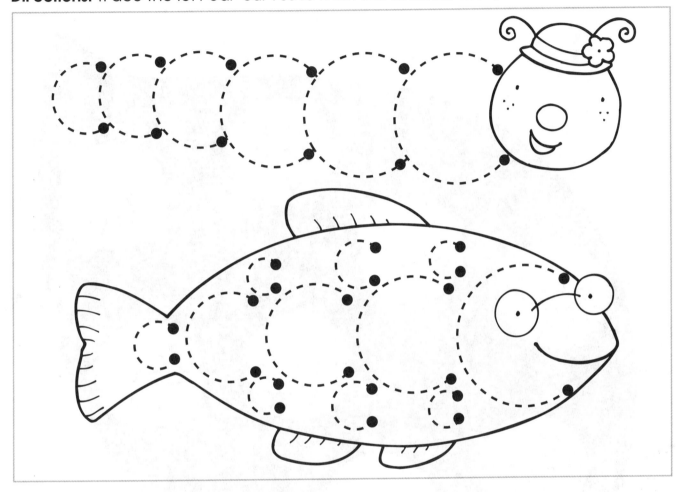

Now, you can write the letters C and c.

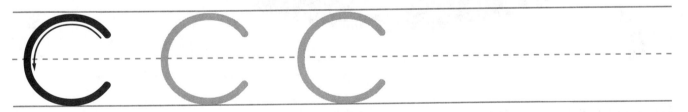

Early Writing Practice

Ladybugs Everywhere!

Directions: Trace the left ear curves to finish the ladybugs. Color the ladybugs.

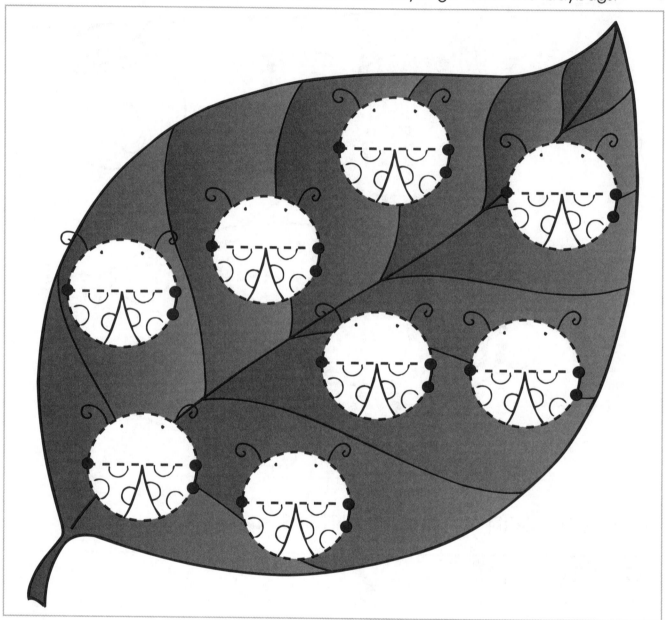

Now, you can write the letter **e**.

Early Writing Practice

Three bees play hide and seek.

2

The bees peek by the tree.

4

Can You See Me?

1

Can you see me?

3

6

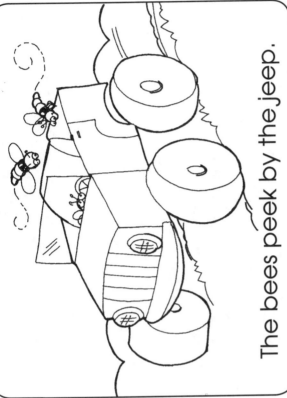

The bees peek by the jeep.

8

Notes to Parents

Directions: First, ask your child to color the mini book. Then, help him or her cut along the dotted lines. Next, have your child arrange the pages in the correct order. Staple the pages together. Read the story out loud to your child.

Extension ideas:
1. Ask your child to count each lowercase **e** that he or she sees.
2. Read each long **Ee** word with your child: **three, bee, bees, me, jeep, see, peek, sleeping, tree.**
3. Say the rhyme, *Eency, Weensy, Spider.*
4. Using **green** playdough, mold an **E** and an **e**.
5. Play hide and seek with your child.

5

Can you see me?

7

See! Bee is sleeping.

39

Early Writing Practice

Leaping Lily Pads!

Directions: Trace the left ear curves to finish the lily pads.

Now, you can write the letter G.

Long and Short Legs

Directions: Draw left ear curves to finish the animals' legs. Color the animals.

Now, you can write the letters **a** and **d**.

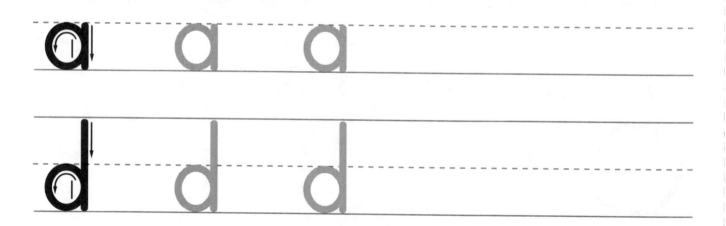

42

Kittens and Yarn

Directions: Trace the lines to the yarn for each kitten.

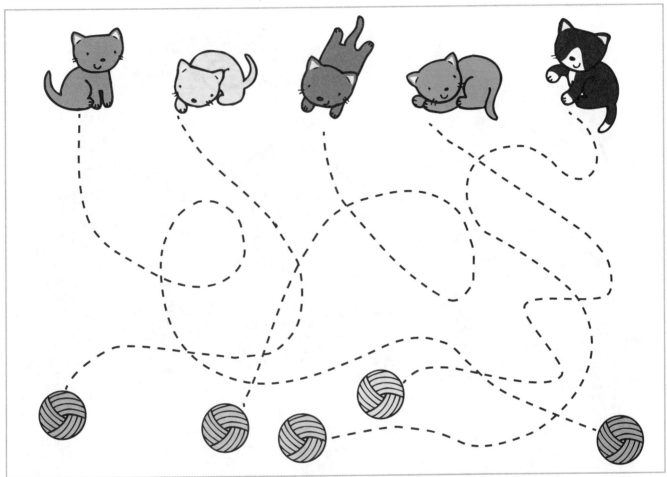

Now, you can write the letters **g** and **q**.

43

Draw Right Ear Strokes

Directions: Start at the • and trace the right ear strokes. Color the apples **red**.

Under the Sea

Directions: Trace the right ear curves to finish the picture. Color the picture.

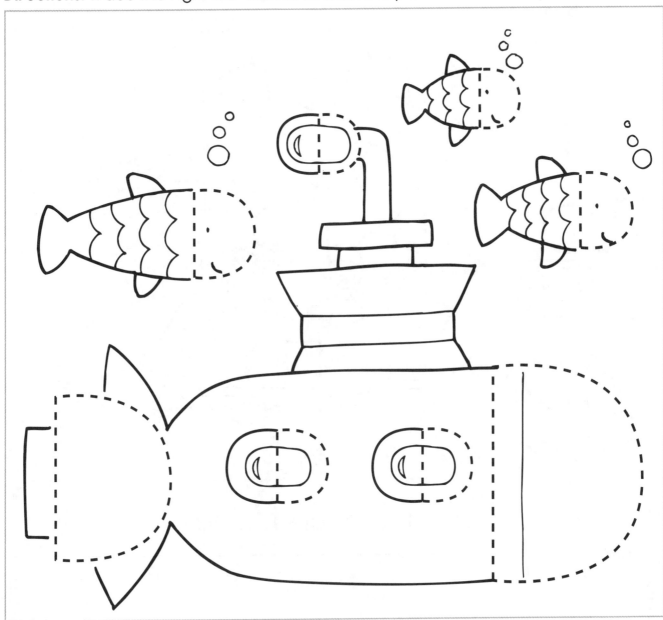

Now, you can write the letter D.

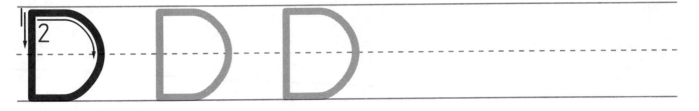

45

Penguin's Hidden Pictures

Directions: Look at the picture. Find all the **P**s and **R**s. Trace each letter with a **blue** crayon.

Now, you can write the letters P and R.

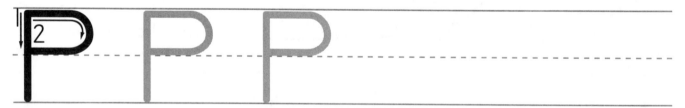

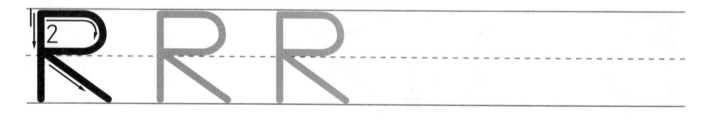

46

Following Directions

Directions: Look at the directions. Draw and color your own butterfly.

1. 2. 3. 4.

Now, you can write the letter B.

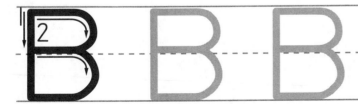

Finish the Owl

Directions: Trace the dotted lines to finish the owl. Can you see a **b** and a **p**? Then, color the owl.

Now, you can write the letters **p** and **b**.

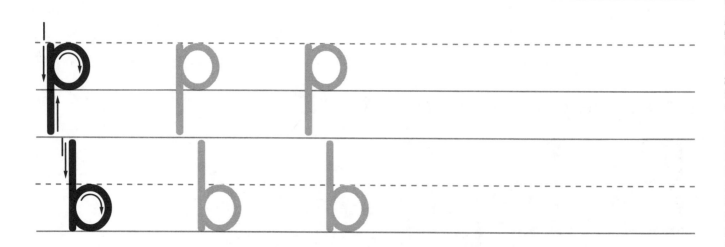

48

Slithering Snakes

Directions: Start at each • and draw curves.

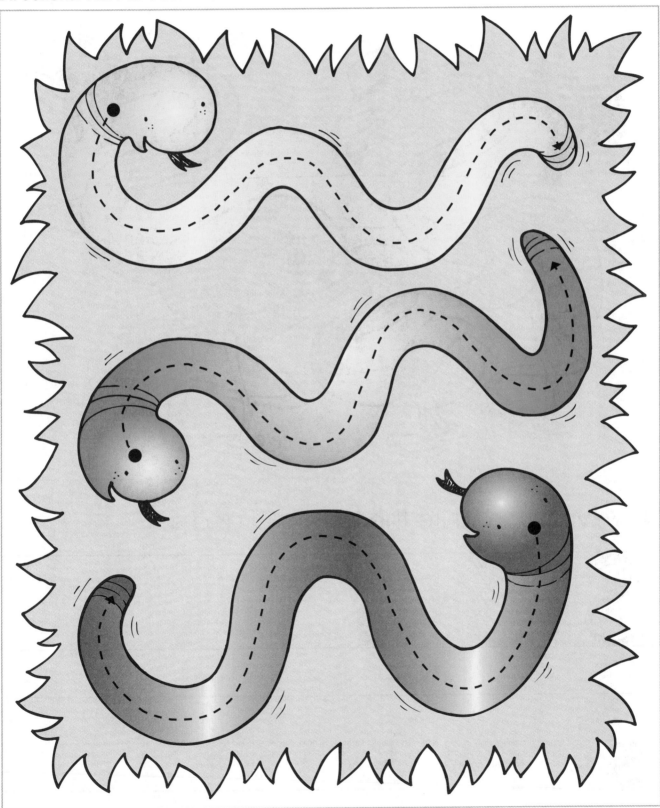

Flamingos

Directions: Trace the left and right ear curves.

Now, you can write the letters S and **s**.

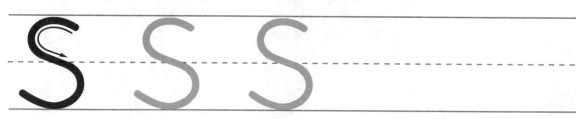

Early Writing Practice

Draw Smile Strokes

Directions: Start at the • and trace all the smile strokes. Color the children.

Early Writing Practice

Flower Garden

Directions: Trace the curves to finish the flowers. Color the picture.

The Wavy Ocean

Directions: Trace smile curves to finish the ocean. Color the picture.

Now, you can write the letters U and **u**.

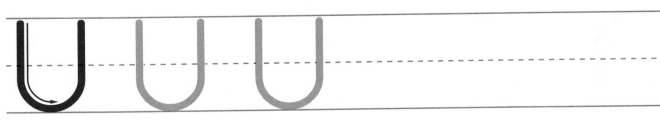

Early Writing Practice

Cute Cottage Dot-to-Dot

Directions: Trace smile curves and connect the dots to finish the cottage.

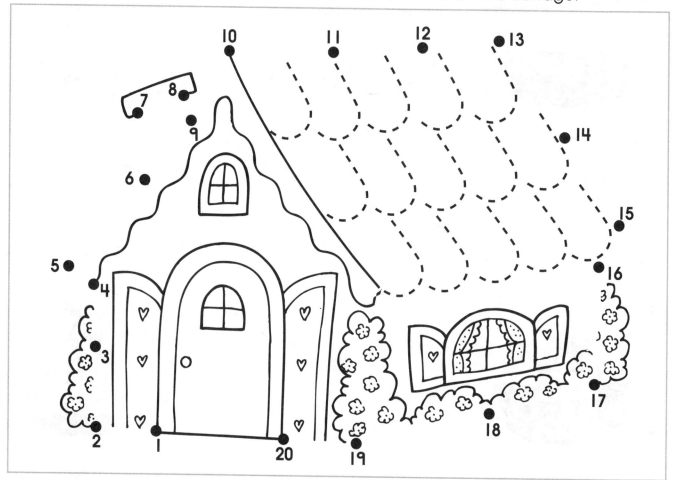

Now, you can write the letters J and j.

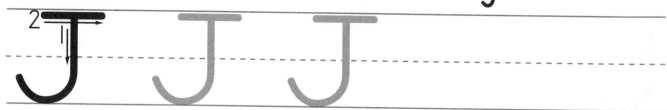

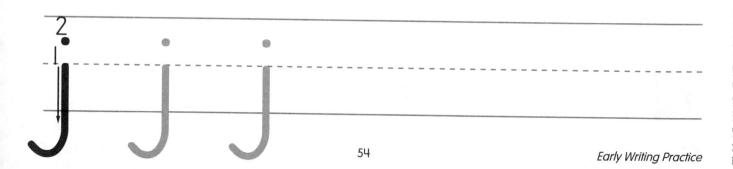

54

Can a jeep jump? No!

2

Can jacks jump? No!

4

Who Can Jump?

1

Can jam and jelly jump? No!

3

55

Early Writing Practice

6

Can Joe and the jack-in-the box jump? No!

8

Notes to Parents

Directions: First, ask your child to color the mini book. Then, help him or her cut along the dotted lines. Next, have your child arrange the pages in the correct order. Staple the pages together. Read the story out loud to your child.

Extension ideas:

1. Ask your child to jump every time he or she sees a **Jj** in the story.
2. Read each **Jj** word with your child: **jump, jeep, jet, jam, jacks, Joe, jelly, jack.**
3. Sing *Jack and Jill* and *John Jacob Jingleheimer Schmidt.*
4. Make gelatin jigglers. Use $2\frac{1}{2}$ cups of boiling water or apple juice, and add two eight-ounce packages of flavored gelatin. Mix together for at least three minutes. Pour into a 9" x 13" pan and refrigerate for at least three hours. Cut out shapes with cookie cutters.

5

Can a jet jump? No!

7

Yes, they can!

Early Writing Practice

Draw Frown Strokes

Directions: Start at the • and trace all the frown strokes. Color the children.

Everyone frowns sometimes!

Directions: Draw a picture of what you look like when you are sad.

Hopping Critters

Directions: Trace the frown curves.

Now, you can write the letters **n** and **m**.

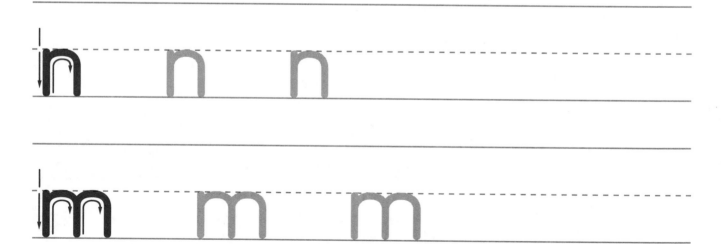

Early Writing Practice

Following Directions

Directions: Look at the directions. Draw and color your own sheep.

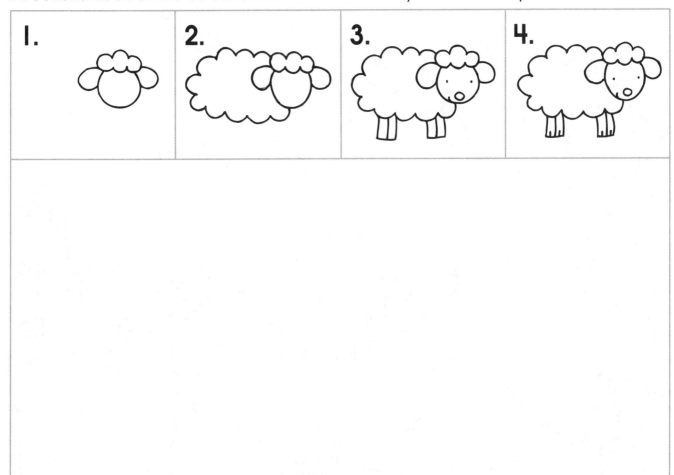

Now, you can write the letters **r** and **h**.

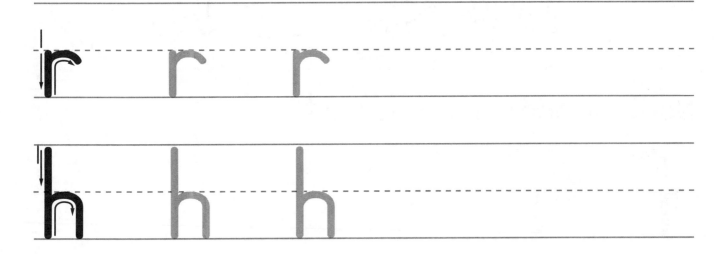

61

Puppy's Hidden Picture

Directions: Look at the picture. Find all the **f**s. Trace each **f** with a **red** crayon.

Now, you can write the letter **f**.

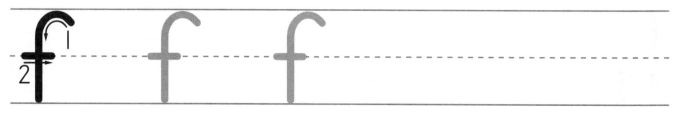

Finish the Peacock

Directions: Draw more feathers for the peacock. Color the peacock.

Early Writing Practice

Practice Printing the Alphabet

Directions: Trace the letters.

Early Writing Practice